I love that you're my

Big Sister

because

I Love You Because Books
www.riverbreezepress.com

To my Big Sister

Love, _____

Date: _____

The best thing about you is your

_____

Thank you for being patient with me when

_____

I remember when we

_____

You should win the grand prize for

_____

You make me feel special when

_____

We would make a great

_____

team

I love when you tell me about

_____

I love when we

_____

together

You taught me how to

_____

I know you love me because

_____

I wish I could

---

as well as
you do

I love that we have the same

_____

You should be the queen of

_____

If you were a plant you would be a

_____

You make me laugh
when you

_____

I wish I had more time to

_____

with you

You make the best

_____

You have inspired me to

_____

If I could give you anything it would be

_____

I would love to go

_____

with you

You have an amazing talent for

_____

I love you
because you are

_____

Made in the USA
Monee, IL
17 July 2025